Pebble® Plus

AFRICAN ANIMALS
Lions

by Catherine Ipcizade
Consulting Editor: Gail Saunders-Smith, PhD

Consultant:
George Wittemyer, PhD
NSF International Postdoctoral Fellow
University of California at Berkeley

Capstone
press®
Mankato, Minnesota

Pebble Plus is published by Capstone Press,
151 Good Counsel Drive, P.O. Box 669, Mankato, Minnesota 56002.
www.capstonepub.com

102010
005961R

Library of Congress Cataloging-in-Publication Data
Ipcizade, Catherine.
    Lions / by Catherine Ipcizade.
        p. cm. — (Pebble plus. African animals)
    Includes bibliographical references and index.
    ISBN-13: 978-1-4296-1248-7 (library binding)
    ISBN-13: 978-1-4296-4882-0 (paperback)
    1. Lions — Africa — Juvenile literature. I. Title. II. Series.
QL737.C23I63 2008
599.757096 — dc22   *5713787*   2007028678

Summary: Discusses lions, their African habitat, food, and behavior.

Editorial Credits
Erika L. Shores, editor; Renée T. Doyle, designer; Laura Manthe, photo researcher

Photo Credits
Afripics.com, 14–15
BigStockPhoto.com/Anke van Wyk, cover, 1, 3 (fur)
Creatas, 20–21
Digital Stock, 4–5
Digital Vision, 6–7, 18–19
iStockphoto/Arman Davtyan, 22; Kristian Sekulic, cover, 1
Peter Arnold Inc./Ferrero J.P./Labat J.M./PHONE, 10–11
Shutterstock/Kristian Sekulic, 9, 12–13; Larsek, 16–17

**The author dedicates this book to her children — her own little lions,
and to her husband — thank you.**

Note to Parents and Teachers

The African Animals set supports national science standards related to life science. This book describes and illustrates lions. The images support early readers in understanding the text. The repetition of words and phrases helps early readers learn new words. This book also introduces early readers to subject-specific vocabulary words, which are defined in the Glossary section. Early readers may need assistance to read some words and to use the Table of Contents, Glossary, Read More, Internet Sites, and Index sections of the book.

Table of Contents

Living in Africa

Lions roam Africa's
grassy savannas, forests,
and dry deserts.

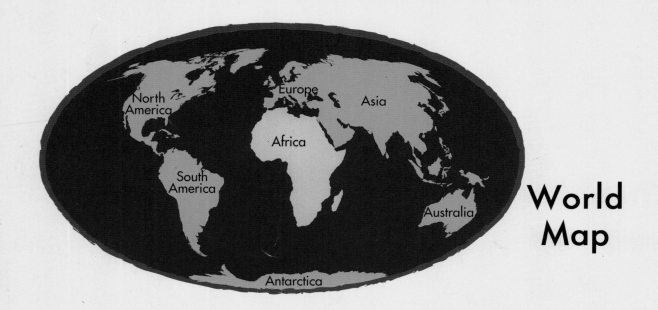

World Map

North America

Europe

Asia

Africa

South America

Australia

Antarctica

Lions live together in prides.

Each pride has its

own territory.

Africa
Map

where lions live

Up Close!

Lions are big cats.

Their ears hear very well.

Their noses smell scents

from far away.

Lions hide in

tall savanna grasses.

Their fur matches the grass.

Male lions have
big, bushy manes.
Manes protect the lions
when they fight.

13

Eating

Female lions hunt.

They catch wildebeests,

zebras, and buffalo to eat.

Lions tear their food
with sharp teeth.
They swallow the meat
without chewing.

Staying Safe

Roar!

Lions protect their territory.

A loud roar warns

other lions to stay away.

Hyenas sometimes attack lions.

Female lions protect their cubs.

Stay safe, lion cubs!

Glossary

cub — a young lion

mane — the long hair along the top and sides of the neck of a male lion

pride — a family of lions

protect — to keep safe

savanna — a flat, grassy plain with few trees

scent — a smell

territory — an area of land that an animal claims as its home

Read More

Cooper, Jason. *Lions*. Eye to Eye with Big Cats. Vero Beach, Fla.: Rourke, 2003.

Rau, Dana Meachen. *Lion in the Grass*. Benchmark Rebus. New York: Marshall Cavendish Benchmark, 2007.

Shively, Julie. *Baby Lion*. San Diego Zoo Animal Library. Nashville, Tenn.: CandyCane Press, 2005.

Internet Sites

FactHound offers a safe, fun way to find Internet sites related to this book. All of the sites on FactHound have been researched by our staff.

Here's how:

1. Visit *www.facthound.com*

2. Choose your grade level.

3. Type in this book ID **1429612487** for age-appropriate sites. You may also browse subjects by clicking on letters, or by clicking on pictures and words.

4. Click on the **Fetch It** button.

FactHound will fetch the best sites for you!

Index

Word Count: 111
Grade: 1
Early-Intervention Level: 16